A poetic memoir like a rush of honesty to the heart (or Gillian Anderson's answerphone.)
— Caroline Bird

I know when I am reading a good book because I swear a lot, silently, inside my head, about the author's intelligence and craft, how it is held so lightly, how it touches you so deeply. I know it's truly good when I want to tell as many people as I can that it is laugh-out loud funny and sad, playful and intelligent - and yes, it's about parenting, and growing up, all the selves we can be in two decades, how sublime we are and how horribly faulty, how this is a book about love. But mostly I just want to tell you – this book is so good. This book is so bloody good
— Clare Shaw

These poems are lyric detonations, excavating constellations of family and strangers, riding the line between reality and lie, holding small worlds but loving big.
— Tishani Doshi

Rhian Elizabeth's poems are personal and playful, tender and fierce. She writes about love, loss and the kindness of strangers. There's an intimacy to these poems, and such honesty and insight, I defy anyone not to be moved.
— Paul Burston

Punchy assured stuff. The writing is clear and direct, leading us effortlessly to all the murk and mulch of life. More please!
— Luke Wright

maybe i'll call gillian anderson

Rhian Elizabeth is a trainee counsellor and a writer. Her debut novel, *Six Pounds Eight Ounces*, was published in 2014 by Seren Books and is currently being adapted for TV, and there are the poetry collections *the last polar bear on earth*, published in 2018 by Parthian Books, and *girls etc.,* by Broken Sleep Books in 2024. Her prose and poetry have been listed in various competitions and prizes and appeared in many magazines and anthologies worldwide, as well as being featured on BBC Radio 4's PM programme. She was named by *The Welsh Agenda* as one of Wales' Rising Stars—one of 30 people working to make Wales better over the next 30 years. She is a Hay Festival Writer at Work and was previously Writer in Residence at the Coracle International Literary Festival in Tranås, Sweden.

Also by Rhian Elizabeth

girls etc. (Broken Sleep Books, 2024)

the last polar bear on earth (Parthian Books, 2018)

Six Pounds Eight Ounces (Seren, 2014)

contents

maybe i'll call gillian anderson	11
drowning on a stranger's couch	13
camden	15
sea glass	17
the bolter	19
escape artist	20
lobster	21
a new and precarious thing	22
the photograph & the man who took it	23
i drank too much and woke up in sweden next to a blonde	25
oyster	26
amsterdam	27
the most pleasing of things	28
the winter the murders stopped	29
glasgow	30
to the girl who said i'll never be happy because i'm too picky	32
mona lisa mona lisa	33
ribbons	34
and what did i teach you, in the end?	36
cry like a bitch	37
boxing day night and my daughter drives us back in the fog	39
i didn't call gillian anderson	40
acknowledgements	43

© 2025, Rhian Elizabeth. All rights reserved; no part of this book may be reproduced by any means without the publisher's permission.

ISBN: 978-1-917617-06-2

The author has asserted their right to be identified as the author of this Work in accordance with the Copyright, Designs and Patents Act 1988

Cover designed by Aaron Kent

Edited and Typeset by Aaron Kent

Broken Sleep Books Ltd
PO BOX 102
Llandysul
SA44 9BG

your enemy is sleeping
— Leonard Cohen

maybe i'll call gillian anderson

Rhian Elizabeth

Broken Sleep Books

maybe i'll call gillian anderson

from the doorstep i watched my daughter
wind down the window of her car,
    put pedal to the floor, fly off
into the vast, calling sky of her life
      and not look back.

this will take some getting used to.
  seeing the carpet clear of dirty laundry,
the absence of a slammed door.
     she took her posters down, leaving me
as redundant as the blu tack that once held up her idols.

my friends tell me i need to keep busy,
   find things to do.
things, they say, that *don't* involve
listening to the carpenters all day long
     and crying.

so off i go to the diy store on the other side of town,
     weeping and humming rainy days and mondays
up the paint aisle before finally settling on a tin
   of nightshade blue, redecorate upon my return,
prise the blu tack off the walls and slowly start to gather
   up the shells left in the empty nest evermore known
      as the spare room.

i order many many things online that i neither want
or need but their impending arrivals give me something
    to look forward to, google hobbies for sad, almost
40 year old women but none of them take
        my meticulous fancy.

  i just wander the house in funereal silence,
though sometimes i find myself standing
    in the empty room, screaming:

    alexa, what the fuck am i meant to do now?

maybe i'll call gillian anderson,
invite her round for a sleepover, put the new sheets
    i bought from ebay on the bed and hope she says,
with a wink, thanks but i think i'd rather sleep in yours,
   hope gillian anderson likes the carpenters
       and crying.

drowning on a stranger's couch

she will watch from the balcony as you descend the steps down
into her pool, you will not be wearing any clothes, you will not
remember her name, the name she told you on the drive across
sweden in her car, you will submerge yourself in the water,
you will see her through the blue green haze of chlorine and sky,
see her blurry silhouette that quivers with the trick of the light,
through the layer of leaves that have dropped from the apple tree
in the yard, you will wonder how long you can hold your breath,
how long you can stay suspended on the bottom, you will think
of how your father, dead twenty years now, taught you to swim
one sunday afternoon in a leisure centre, a thousand miles away
from here,

she will bring you a towel, you will put your clothes back on,
you will stay the morning, the afternoon, the evening, she will
show you around the grand house, you will pick up and put down
antiques like an interested child, she will talk about her paintings,
you will pause and tilt your head at the ones on easels waiting for
a brush to finish the sentence, she will cook you a meal of herring
and potatoes and bread, she will watch you eat, she will tell you
about her husband who died, her sons who moved out long ago,
one of them works in the city, he does not visit, she has a
granddaughter who plays the violin very well but she does not
visit either, she will ask if you are full, she will ask if you have
had enough, she will take away your plate,

you will sit in her conservatory with the windows pushed wide
open, the night will be hot, you will close your eyes, you will

think about the pool outside, you will think of yourself weightless
on the bottom, you will listen to the crickets singing, they live on
the lake in the distance, the great lake is vättern or sommen, you
aren't sure which, this she told you on the drive across sweden
in her car too but you had your head out of the window like a dog,
you will wonder if this is a mistake, you make bad decisions,
she will bring you lemon iced tea, you will feel tired, she will
convince you to stay the night on the massive old couch, you
will dream about your father there, you will give him a new face,
you will give him a new voice, you will no longer remember
the actual ones he had, you will dream about swimming in vättern
or sommen, you will dream you are drowning,

you will wake up with a blanket over you that wasn't there when
you fell asleep, you will be made fresh coffee, you will be served
eggs and bacon, the bread from last night toasted, you will be
gifted a painting of a cat, the one you said you liked when she
showed it to you yesterday, she will remind you to fasten your
seatbelt before she will start the car, she will drive you back
across sweden to the place where you are staying, she will wave
you goodbye with the saddest face you have ever seen, you will
feel sorry for her, you will think she is very lonely, you will never
write the letter you vow you will write when you eventually
return home to wales a few weeks later, the thank you to the
stranger who misses being a mother, from the girl who misses
being a daughter.

camden

dear you whoever you are,

you are not real   then again neither am i   anymore
i have a fake ID but no one ever checks it   they say
   i am a very smart person   who is doing very dumb things
         or at least i *was* a smart person before   i disappointed
   my mother   did i ever tell you that, at the start of high school,
         they put me in a special club for gifted kids?   can you
imagine that, now? me? no one would believe it   last night
i threw up in a bin on shaftesbury avenue
   we went to see rachel stamp again, they're my favourite band
  we sort of follow them around   david ryder prangley is a god
            and we are his disciples
london is mad though   the tube scares me   i am re-remembering
                  an argument with my mother
i don't eat very much but on the bright side i've lost loads of weight
you can see my ribs!
                  i fall in love with every single girl i meet, it seems
   it is the first day of november   and there is no heating
         in the place where we're staying,
under my inherited quilt i dream about cakes with thick thick icing
   and girls with warm warm hands
   i can't go home right now or maybe   ever
i got my clit pierced   susanna is still selling her body,
      i told her that her mind is golden
   and then we kissed a bit on a bench in phoenix garden,
but i'm ashamed to say i couldn't stop
thinking about where her lips had been   the tongue is a doormat

                          and they wipe their feet
  i don't know it yet
  but in less than eighteen months' time i will be a mother!
   i am fifteen years old
i remember in junior school
       our teacher taught us how to properly write a letter, how
to put the address in the top right hand corner
    and the dear whoever on the left   then you sign off
      with a yours sincerely   or a yours hopefully
i can't remember which is appropriate   for an imaginary friend
  you see, i *have* gone dumb!   if you could write me back,
that would be nice   i have broken my wrist so
i'll stop writing now,   if you don't mind

yours sincerely or

yours hopefully

sea glass

i don't understand

how they were once bottles
& plates & all manner
of unremarkable objects,
ugly lost things tossed
around the ocean for centuries,
maybe they came from shipwrecks
sunk by storms,
but now they're pretty jewels
tucked inside your jeans pocket.

        i don't understand a lot of things.

you say you want to remember
this day, this beach, this kiss,
you say you will take an apple
green triangular piece & turn
it into a necklace for me
but your efforts will be wasted.

        i will not wear it.

i don't mean to come across
as unsentimental, it's just
that i fear i can never be
fashioned into something
beautiful, however many
tides come in or out

    & however hard you might want to try.

i want to live inside your jeans pocket,
believe me, but i also don't want
to remember the look on your face

    when i sink the ship.

the bolter

when a friend tells me over coffee and bagels
*it's time, you need to stand on your own two
feet,* i can't help think of your first pair of
shoes. clarks shoe shop, and you screaming
and squirming as the poor young boy struggled
like the prince in cinderella trying to cajole them
onto the wrong sister's foot. how they gave you
a new found confidence when you eventually
came round to the idea of them.

                                     not that you needed it.
as soon as you could walk you had the inclination
to bolt and there was i, forever yanking you back
on your reins like you were an over-excited pup.
elvis' were blue suede and dorothy's were ruby red.

lace them tight, darling –
you're finally free to run

escape artist

when i was a child my sleepwalking
was an almost nightly occurrence.
my mother would find me standing on the bottom step
of our garden, a little lost ghost in a nightgown,
paper thin against the elements on those welsh valleys nights.
then there was the time she caught me pissing
in the living room plant pot, the time i toppled books
and shelves and chairs during a rare stay
with my older brother in his fancy windsor apartment,
and i was once rescued by a neighbour
from the middle of the road where i was staring,
just staring,
at nothing in the darkness, all this despite the locks fixed
to my windows and doors –
i was an escape artist in a pair of fluffy pink slippers.
sometimes i will do it now, but not very often, and only
when i am in a strange place, strange
in the sense that the city outside the window is not mine,
the bed is not mine,
and the person next to me is not mine either, not really,
because people never are, are they? and because love
oh love is the strangest of all places,
the place where the sleeping dream
and the dreamers walk

lobster

you asked me
what i thought
the soul looked
like and i couldn't
be bothered to think
of something intelligent
so i just took
my clothes off

when we were together
i felt like a lobster drifting
in a restaurant tank
watching you popping
the champagne and having
a great time while i
waited to die
and that's a terrible thing
to say i know but a lot
of time has passed

and i can see from your
instagram posts that you
are happy now and have
found someone who probably
tells you *exactly* what the soul
looks like every night in
exquisite detail while i
knock my pincers futilely
against the glass.

a new and precarious thing

the night you fell through the front door *that* night the night
you threw up in your doc martens *that* night the night i scooped

the sick out of your doc martens with my bare hands *that* night
the night you heaved all your gossip out in a phlegmy stream

of purple vodka across the bathroom floor *that* night the night your
brain was spinning like a disco ball and the patterns on the ceiling

were turning like catherine wheels *that* night the night you swore
you'd never drink again and i thought yeah okay we'll see *that* night

the night i tucked you under your covers *that* night the night you
let me rub your back like i used to when i was needed to there there

a scary dream *that* night the night i came in and out of your room when
you fell asleep to check you were breathing like i did in the very very

first days of you when your breathing was a new and precarious thing
that night the night you were eighteen but a babe again *that night*

the night i was a mother again.

the photograph & the man who took it

what did you do with the photograph,
        the one you took of me back
in the days of setting myself on fire

        & disposable cameras?

i think about you carrying it in your trouser
        pocket up to the kiosk in the supermarket,
sliding it across the counter

        i think about someone
in a long white coat & the look on their face
        when the film develops - - -

their lack of conscience
        & yours - - -

i think about how i skipped school
        how, in the train toilet, i changed out of my uniform
into a brand new dress, trying to look older
        but you knew *exactly* how old i was

you took that dress off
        with the confidence of a man
who'd taken off
        a hundred dresses

i think about the bed & the satin sheets,
        the nightstand next to it, the reading lamp
& the alarm clock & the bottle of cologne,
        the pair of glasses on top of an open book - - -

i was a child
        in a grown up's bedroom   - - -

i think about that photograph all the time
        although i think of you

very little

i just dream
        about breaking into your house & stealing it
except all i find when i climb through your kitchen window
        & open door   after door after door

is
empty rooms

if someone took a photograph of my daughter like that
i would kill them
i would fucking kill them

do you still look at it?
        am i smiling?

to this day i blame myself
        even though i was not the one
who pressed the shutter.

i drank too much and woke up in sweden next to a blonde

if i could speak your language
i'd ask you to leave so that
i might be afforded the dignity
of a private death as i slowly
drown in this whiskey sea
of shame, but i can't.
the one and only word i know
in swedish is *tack* which means,
of all unhelpful things, *thank you*.
so i just rush you out the door into
the blinding sunlight with your shoes
in one hand, a mug of steaming black
coffee in the other, and send you on
your way with an awkward hug
and a compliment i can't even
remember if you deserve...
tack!

oyster

somewhere, in a university dormitory,

    boxes have been unpacked, a string of fairy lights

hangs over a bed where a stuffed japanese cat

    takes pride of place, a set of keys on a fob that says

fuck the patriarchy dangles off the edge of a desk

    strewn with books and pens, a pack of benson and hedges,

a mug of peppermint tea gone cold

    and a letter from a mother left unopened, taylor swift

is playing on spotify, the world is an oyster,

    and my daughter is pulling a face as she puts her makeup on,

unaware of how beautiful she is,

    how much her mother misses her.

amsterdam

the spring i woke to find my pillowcase stained
the colour of red wine, after i caught glandular
fever from the sneezing girl in the toilets of a club,
was the spring i did the most damage. i was flying
downhill on my grandmother's steep street when
the brakes on my bike went and the world imploded,
except my grandmother had been dead for two years
and, after the funeral, when the car took her away
from the house i had known all my life, i never set foot
on that street again, and i can't ride a bike, so that is all
   a lie,
the truth of that spring is more complicated, much simpler
–girl loses her father, girl loses her mind.
i wrapped myself in barbed wire so that no one
would touch me, and if they did and they bled i laughed
and told them it served them right.
time softens a person, i think, as
   i lie,
twenty years later, covered in bubbles,
alone in the bathtub of an amsterdam hotel.

the most pleasing of things

i can still remember my grandmother's telephone number,
an old landline disconnected way back in the nineties,
but not the feel of her hand gripping mine as we cross
the busy main road of my childhood town, even though
i search for its warmth in my vault of memories like i'm
a burglar ransacking my own jewellery drawer.
what i'm trying to say is that memory is a contemptuous
old bitch. she likes to unearth the shameful fossils i try
to bury on the beach of my mind, their contours revealing
at any given, unwelcome moment things like... all details
of the night i fell asleep as i was going down on the girl
who was notoriously hard to please, how i woke up
to find her staring at me with what the fuck eyes,
and even though the pleasing of that girl *was* the most
pleasing of things, i would prefer to forget that blip
in performance, prefer to forget all the threesomes,
the foursomes, the fivesomes, the never-gonna-happen-
rhian-somes, the absolute shitstorm of my past,
but she won't let me. and yet other times she's a bouncer
flexing her muscles at the door of the club. i want in,
want to waltz with my father who is inside waiting
for me on the dancefloor, to remember his voice,
to feel his arms around me as he spins me about to a song
we both know, but she pushes her heavy hand against
my chest. i turn around and leave. my father dances alone.

the winter the murders stopped

i went to the christmas party dressed as a reindeer,
        top floor apartment by the river,
spilled my manhattan over her and her couch, cold collarbones,
        cold leather, walked home
through the glacial streets drenched in stars, coat slick
        with sleet and regret,

        i feel like a photograph yellowing.

        i miss hearing the creak of my daughter's bedframe
in the middle of the night, miss being summoned
        for glasses of water she could easily
get herself, and now my house is filled
        with spiders, since there is
no one here afraid of them,

        asking me to kill for them, anymore.

glasgow

when the chef made me cry you held me and said,
in cracked english that somehow lost none of its
tenderness during the scuffle of translation,
that *real men don't shout at girls.*
we both hated the guy.
the two of us worked like dogs in the hotel kitchen
that summer while he erupted over the various things
we were doing wrong or not fast enough. me,
barely sixteen years of age, four hundred miles away
from home and you, a boy from estonia who couldn't
have been much older, but my hands were soft and yours
had already seen half the world by the time
they were holding mine over the sink
under a jet of cold water.

you taught me how to steer a kayak,
watched me slice through the surface of loch tay
the way that knife sliced through my skin.
you were holding my hand again when we snuck
into the grand hall and drank the champagne
left over from a wedding. it felt like we had crept
into someone's dream while they were sleeping.
you showed me how to pitch a tent the night
we slept under a sky of uncountable stars
on the ben lawers mountains,
how to gut a fish, how to sweat an onion,
how to not kill myself
every time i picked up a knife.

on one of your days off you took the bus
into glasgow and brought me back a stuffed
polar bear that i still have.
and then one morning,
some weeks after the bear,
i heard from one of the housekeepers
you'd caught that same bus in the dead of night,
rode out to some other hotel in some other country,
onto some other adventure. you left me alone
with the chef who smashed plates, who threw vats of soup
at the walls and made me clean it up, who called me stupid,
and other names you said real men don't call girls
but by then you'd also taught me how to say
fuck you in estonian, taught me not to cry.

to the girl who said i'll never be happy because i'm too picky

you preferred orange juice to apple.
this, i discovered,
the morning after
the night i had to sleep in the spare room
because your breathing reminded me of my
grandmother's old fashioned kettle whistling
in the kitchen whenever she made herself
a cup of tea. after that,
just to prove my unfastidious-ness,
i took to bringing my own carton of apple juice
round for breakfast, and even tried
looking past the fact you never laughed at my
leave the gun, take the cannoli
joke when i handed you the bag of pastries
in the italian bakery.

who the fuck
hasn't seen the godfather?

and who the fuck
doesn't know every single word
to barbra streisand's
the way we were?

i put up with a lot.

oh, and by the way,
i'd never dated someone
shorter than me before i met you

but i never looked down on you,
not even for that.

mona lisa mona lisa

you are everything that is good in this world

and at times   – *all* of the time –

it is confusing that you came from me

   i study your face the way scientists
study famous paintings with infrared technology

                        underneath the mona lisa they found

                        another mona lisa, and that is what *i*

                        am doing when i look at you,

                        searching for the painting behind

                        the painting, trying to find the me

                        that is in you

   you're the only thing
i ever did right.

ribbons

once,
in the middle of the night
when i was very very drunk
and not wearing any trousers,
or had lost my trousers,
i walked home from a party to the wrong house.
i rocked up
swaying,
soaked to the bone,
on the doorstep of the place i must've forgotten
i'd moved out of three years before,
and was confused when the person
who answered the door was not my girlfriend
who had broken up with me,
also three years before,
but a pissed off old lady who'd been extracted
from her warm bed by my hammering
and yelling.
that was also the night i flagged down
a random car on the highway and got in,
something
i am now always telling my daughter
never *ever* to do,
and if i close my eyes tight enough
i can still see the windscreen wipers dancing
through the rain, see his fat fingers wrapped
around the steering wheel,
the hairs on his knuckles twirling

like little ribbons
in the breeze
from his rolled down window,
feel my wet thighs pasting themselves
to the leather passenger seat,
hear the hot air roar
from the heater he winds on
as i shiver and my teeth chatter.
and this poem
doesn't have an awful ending,
except perhaps to say
that i have yet to find my way home,
or is me being such a mess, still,
the reason why no one ever lets me in
when i bang on their door?

and what did i teach you, in the end?

i guess i always felt more
like the teenage babysitter,
dubiously holding down
the fort until the parents
returned

except i was the mother,
and no one was coming
to drive me
home.

cry like a bitch

i sit in the tattooist's chair
and tell him to give me something
i will regret in three months' time

these days i am like this, impulsive,
or at least i am in the way an almost
40 year old woman who has given up
drinking alcohol and fucking just about
every person she meets who is nice to her
is

in truth i gave up the second thing a very long time ago
and now the first thing i do in the mornings when
i wake up is drink a full fat can of coke in protest

i know it will rot my insides

but i can't give it up either, like a lover who you know
will fuck you over eventually but there you are cracking

the top of the can in your silk pyjamas and slippers, looking
out the patio windows at the happy little birds on the feeder

i still listen to rachel stamp
but occasionally when i'm eating
my muesli i will listen to schubert,
and then just when i think i've finally
got living down to a science i find

a scrunchie down the back
of the radiator in my daughter's
old bedroom
(i clean a lot now)
and cry like a bitch

she says i need to stop writing about her,
and i will, when i've gotten used
to the way of things

i blinked

i just fucking blinked.

boxing day night and my daughter drives us back in the fog

it is only now i see it,
as i look across at you
gripping the steering
wheel for dear life, that
our roles have reversed,
christmas is done with,
and i cannot keep you safe
any more than your headlights
can penetrate the miasma
of white ahead of us

it's been a journey, kid
but we did it

we made it home.

i didn't call gillian anderson

> i continued at night school,
> meditated a shit load
> and thought about very deep
> and very trivial things for hours
> on my shakti mat,

caught the coach to edinburgh and cried when iris dement
sang "my life" in the concert hall under the smog of the stage
lights, her small voice like a pain you can't fathom but a pain
you know, went back to my hotel room, ate some pistachios
on the bed and thought about how things had changed since
i was first in scotland all those years ago, thought about that
teenage girl, how much she had grown, how much she had not,
wept for her, laughed at her, stepped out the next morning onto
the freezing pavements of the old town into a cloud of smoke
and coffee and books,

> in london i took the circle line and saw friends
> i hadn't seen in years, when they asked me how
> it is now that my daughter has left home i tried
> to explain that it's kind of like losing a pet,
> like your beloved cat escaping through an open
> window, you don't understand how they could
> just up and leave, you were the best of friends,
> you did everything for that little shit but now
> they rarely even call, you learn to swallow
> your pride, you must think of them out there
> in the world on their own and just hope that
> they are safe, that they are happy, that someone
> is feeding them, or that they are at least feeding
> themselves occasionally,

i could tape a poster to a lamppost, make an appeal,

                but my daughter would not want to come home,

she is not lost, she is free,

                i didn't call gillian anderson in the end
                because i learned a long time ago that
                beautiful women aren't the solution
                to your problems and because, you know,
                i don't have her fucking phone number.

acknowledgements

Thank you

Aaron, Stu and everyone at Broken Sleep Books.

Clare Potter, Louise Walsh, Catrin Kean, Rebecca Parfitt, Fizzy Oppe, Mark Blayney, Phil Jones, Ben and Susie Wildsmith, Jon Gower, Hanan Issa, Eleanor Shaw, Taz Rahman, Robin Ganderton, Clare Shaw and Caroline Wyatt.

Hay Festival and, in particular, Tiffany Murray - love ya, Nanna.

Rachel Trezise - for writing the truth about our lives, about who we are and where we come from, for In and Out of The Goldfish Bowl, a book I carried around in my rucksack all those years ago, a book that helped me immensely, and for inspiring me more than you know and more than I will ever tell you in person.

Leanne Wood - for your kindness and support when I needed it the most. Diolch.

Caroline Bird, Tishani Doshi, Paul Burston, Luke Wright and Clare Shaw (again) - I am so so grateful for your extraordinarily generous endorsements of this book. It's completely ridiculous and wonderful and baffling to me when writers I love and read and admire say nice things about my stuff.

Gillian Anderson - for not suing me (yet).

Finally, and most importantly, to Scout - I love you and I'm proud of you. And if it wasn't for you, where the fuck would I be?

LAY OUT YOUR UNREST

www.ingramcontent.com/pod-product-compliance
Lightning Source LLC
LaVergne TN
LVHW091103030725
815301LV00006B/377